HOW TO USE COMPUTER AND LOCAL BUSINESS
TO
EMPLOY YOURSELF

BY
MARC MONTGOMERY

PART ONE

SECTION ONE

GO WHERE MONEY IS

In section two you will learn and train yourself on how to go after your money which is in the pockets of your prospects. You will have the know-how about seeking and approaching them; and then convincing them to spend their money on your product or service. In this section you will learn about home businesses you can start on shoestring budget. You will need to choose the kind of business you feel interested in and then give it your all to ensure its success. Whatever you do never do half things or in a half hearted manner. Do not try to mix what you learn here with other plans or methods which may cause you to replace what you learned here with something else. What I have written works and it is complete by itself. You can add your extras on the condition that you have started making money and you see the need to add some technique or method to leverage what is already working for you. Most importantly, never undertake to pursue more than one business until your first choice if running in full steam and that it can continue running well when you attend to the second business you want to start. Do not try to be like a man who tries to ride two horses at the same time. Ever remember that; 'single-mindedness guarantees success.' From now on you will need to align your life, attitude, beliefs and efforts to all the words of wisdom you hear about even if you do not fully believe in them. The reason is if you go against the words of wisdom you will waste years of your life learning from your mistakes. So do make a firm decision to live literally according to the words of wisdom you become aware of. After wasting time learning the hard way you will eventually decide to live by them because of your unhappy experiences. If you are youthful or naive you are likely to follow your own beliefs and convictions because you are likely yet filled with yourself despite the fact that you do not have any huge success to prove the effectiveness of your beliefs which are contrary to the words of wisdom. As a matter of rule, every time you are faced with a decision do check what idioms, proverbs and other words of wisdom say and then decide to follow their advice instead of following your own unproven wit.

HOW I OVERCAME SHYNESS

Since this is not a get rich quick scheme, you will need to come down to earth, if you thought you were going to get a press button method of making money. This method is actually about creating a job for you which is not an easy task for some people. The difficult part will be to approach people if you are, by nature, a reserved person; the kind of a person who is generally sensitive to issues and the action or responses of others. When I got my first job at the bank I felt fine and there was no pressure from anyone to force me to do anything which was against my nature or liking. It was when I got my second job as an insurance representative that I felt the heaviness of working for a company. My job was to convince people to buy insurance policies from me so that I could get paid the commission at the end of the month.

Because of my reserved and sensitive nature the idea of approaching strangers and convincing them to apply for insurance was very difficult to say the least. It was an uphill struggle to approach any one to sell to. For about two months I never made a any single sale because I would sit under a shade and try to convince myself that I needed to approach people. Fortunately, my manager was pushing me to bring business but he was not fighting me. Many times I thought of giving up, but the fact that I saw fellow workers bringing business every week without fail and making huge commissions; and the fact that I had stayed without work for almost two years after I left my bank job made decide to stick in this new job. Again, I had prayed for a job and three times I was encouraged or advised by people who asked me to join insurance work rather than wait for the job I would feel comfortable with. When the third person came to my home to specially ask me to join insurance I was became somehow convinced that it was God answering my prayer for work. That is how I joined the insurance company and started to sell insurance. The third person who advised me to work for an insurance company was an insurance representative also.

On the third month I started to bring little business I had managed to get strangers to sign up for insurance through me. At the end of the month i got a little pay but it was enough encouragement and motivation to me. It was about four months when I started to begin to enjoy going after strangers to sell them insurance policy. The reason was that I began to see myself as the helper of people to cause them to avoid living their lives without an insurance policy. As I became more interested in selling policies I started to device my own techniques and manner of approach and convincing that propelled me to become somehow of an expert. I started teaching new insurance workers the skills that were working for me and they were grateful for my assistance and guidance.

It was about a year and half when I started my own insurance brokering by opening my own insurance office where I would sell insurance using my own representatives so that I stop going to people, but rather, send my trained representatives to get business for me. Every Monday I would hold motivational meetings where I would encourage, teach and solve the problems and objections my workers faced when selling insurance for my brokering company. In just two short months I crossed R50.000 in commissions. My workers seemed to have caught the spirit of being the treasured helpers of mankind.

WHAT I TEACH WORKS

What I teach in this publication is what worked for me and them. It is not about what is supposed to work; but what actually worked not only for me but also for those I taught these sales methods to. The good thing about selling is that you will never have to wait for a vacancy to become available and hope that you land the job for which you are competing for with many others. The reason I wrote this publication is to give people who are waiting for vacancies to stop waiting for what they do not know when it will become available to them; and to start making things happen for them and their loved ones. Admittedly, it is going to be a painful struggle for those who have sensitive nature and do not like talking to people they do not know, and worse, to try to convince them to part with their money in exchange for his product or service. But, it is the training and the willingness to hold on until your nature is turned around and you begin to enjoy freelancing as your preferred work. Freelancing is pitiful from the outside view but very attractive from the inside when going to strangers has turned into joy and positive anticipation; and you see your duty as a work of salvation from undesired circumstances and lack. Which means it is all in the mind.

START A NEW HABIT

It is very unpleasant or uncomfortable to start any new habit. The secret is to fight or force your being to start a new habit of selling, however unpleasant it may be. And later that habit you started will begin to make you. You must keep at it until the new habit of going to strangers and convincing them to spend money on what you want them to becomes a joy for you. You must fight to reach the state of feeling and believing that you are a very important source of solutions to people's needs and convenience around you; and this attitude will spur you on to approach as many people as possible, which means more money for you.

As a freelancer you work at your own pace, you determine how much you want to make per month. You also have the opportunity to come up with your own innovative means to increase the number of your clients. In short the sky is the limit when you work as a Representative for any company or yourself. True, from the outside the work is very much unattractive and seemed to be for people who are less knowledge-able or losers of some sort; but the money they make is hard to believe. Through freelancing you have the power to start making things happen for you and your loved ones while others are waiting for unpredictable vacancies. Sales work is the only work where there is always a room for one more person to join. There will never be a time when the door of self employment will be shut for anyone who wants to enter the life of making money through sales of products or services. And unlike countless money making methods that are advertised on the Internet and newspapers that do not work in most cases, this SELF HELP money making system creates the real job, which will reward anyone who will put in the necessary effort and skills as taught in this publication.

SECTION TWO

HOW TO PROSPECT FOR CLIENTS:

The idea here is to come up with a list of the people you will start your business with; by selling to them. Buy a diary or exercise book. Now write the names of 100 working people you know presently and from the past. You need to write names and telephone numbers of their work place or their cell numbers. It should be people who know you; people who will not be offended that you called them. In your book, categorize their names by their profession or places of work. When you see the word GARAGE below you will need to write under that category all the people you know who work at all garages you know as mechanics, clerks and managers, etc. Do not be in a hurry because you are trying to get your memory to aid you with as much recall as possible. When you finished recalling and writing down all names get a phone directory and start writing phone numbers of their homes or work place next to each name. Do not look into directory while you are brainstorming / recalling the names of the people. Below are the categories I have noted for you:

1. Garages
2. Hospitals (doctors, nurses, drivers and cleaners)
3. Surgeries
4. Banks
5. Filling stations
6. Taxi and bus drivers and those who work with them
7. Internet café workers
8. People who work in various government departments
9. Correctional service
10. Domestic workers
11. Miners
12. Insurance workers
13. Print and media
14. Army
15. Teachers (crèche, primary, high schools, colleges, tertiary)
16. Universities workers
17. Carpenters, plumbers, painters
18. Gardeners, tree fellers
19. Supermarket workers

20. Porters
21. Labour workers
22. Widows and widowers
23. Sports: supporters and players
24. Casino workers
25. Hotel, hostel, Bed and breakfast
26. Hawkers (ice cream, clothes, food vendors, etc.)
27. Metro rail workers
28. Police service
29. Roads workers
30. Take away shops workers
31. Fried chicken, Pizza, meat outlets workers
32. Pharmacy
33. Bookshops

34. Magazine and newspaper sellers
35. Gyms workers
36. Gym enthusiasts
37. Parks and recreational centres workers
38. Municipal workers
39. Community policing workers
40. Aged people who use cell phones
41. Radio stations workers and DJ's
42. Factory (clothing, bedding, cars, milk, foods)
43. Beverages' companies
44. Electronics shops
45. Pawn / charity shops
46. Shoe sellers
47. Shoe repairs
48. Sowing and tailoring
49. Zoo / museums
50. Hospice
51. People who work with animals
52. Game rangers and other workers
53. Security officers
54. Beauty shop workers

55. Salon workers
56. Storage services workers
57. Barbers / hair cutting biz
58. Singers/dancers
59. Building construction workers
60. Furniture shops
61. Recyclers
62. Clothes shops
63. Importers and exporters
64. Courier services workers
65. Secretarial services
66. Fruit shop
67. Vegetable shops
68. Cell phone shops
69. Cell phone repairs
70. Computer sales / repairs
71. Farm workers
72. Fence and gates workers
73. Towing services
74. Second hand car shop workers
75. New car dealers works
76. Car wash
77. Hotel workers (drivers, waiters, chefs, etc.)
78. Gamblers, bettors, lotto participants
79. Distributors
80. Wholesale workers

81. Retail workers
82. Manufacturers
83. Street food vendors
84. Flea market workers

If you recall / know 3 people from each category you will have over 250 prospective customers.
Now that you have a list of potential clients to monetize you will need to schedule the names by dates you will see them personally at their work places. You will

also need to group them according to their locations so that you see six or more per day without too much travelling between them. This is the best and very efficient approach which is used by large Insurance companies to amass fortunes for themselves month after month.

HOW TO DEAL WITH POTENTIAL CLIENTS:

First, you set an appointment for your service / product presentation. Second, you arrive 15 minutes before the appointment time. Third, you present your service or product to your potential client. Four, you close the sale. Never arrive after appointed time. You can also employ Call Centre style to call your potential clients on their phone. When you speak on the phone you should sound like a professional who knows what he is talking about without hesitations and forgetting some parts because your customers will pick it up instantly and will lose interest just as soon.

PRACTISE PRESENTATION SKILL:

Spend about a week rehearsing your opening lines when you first meet a client face to face or over the phone. Do not speak things from yourself or your way but do follow the guide lines in this publication. Practice by pretending to meet a client. Talk to imaginary him or her, and also try to play his part concerning his responses to your presentation. Namely: 1. introducing yourself and your product. 2. Setting an appointment. 3. Presenting your service. 4. Handling imaginary objections from prospects. 5. Closing the sale. 6. Getting three referrals from every person you presented your service to; regardless of whether he bought from you or not

AN EXAMPLE OF SETTING AN APPOINTMENT:

Your first line when you meet a potential prospect or on the phone: "Hello! How are you? My name is... (Say your name) ... from Frank Research, Johannesburg. (Say the assumed name you intend to register as soon as you get money if you presently have none). I would like to tell you about our interesting self help / educational programs which are benefiting / have benefited many people / our clients / students (Note: choose appropriate words for your presentation.) However, you are the one who will decide. Can I see you tomorrow at 3:00 PM or

Friday at 10.00 AM? (Then wait for him to tell the right time and day convenient for him. When he gives the appointment write it down right in front of him so that he knows you mean business. Thank him for his time and leave. Do not talk about the weather and other time wasting topic unless it is him who starts such conversation).

AN EXAMPLE OF PRESENTATION:

When you meet your potential client for the presentation of your product or service you get down to presentation business (this is a guide line which can be used for various products' sales or services): "Mr. Baker, have you noticed the influx of students to universities has reached the highest proportions since our new democracy so much that thousands of students who have passed their metric fail to be admitted? And the admission preference is given to the students who have passed well than others. The intake list starts with distinction passes to lower until the set number of intake is reached; which leaves two third of applicants outside. This tells you and me that for your high school child to be admitted at university he or she will need to beat two thirds of all fellow applicants for an admission. Now our company has done something to help the parents who really do not wish to leave the success of their children's successful university entry to chance.

The way we do it is by introducing our unique study method which has proven to produce powerful results for any average student. This study method increases grades by over 40%. This is enough to put any student in the first one third of possible admission by the universities. (This saying deals with potential objections before they rise from Mr. Baker) Mr. Baker, your child will love our system because it does not require rote learning, mnemonics, meditations or any methods used by other less effective systems on the market today. Again, a student can implement the method without any external help from a parent. (Now it is time to close the sale). Our study method costs R850.00 which includes two months email or telephone support in case your child needs some assistance with any issue. (Note: Charge more if you have to take the manuals to your client for your time and transportation.) Should your child indicate that he needs the actual assistance of being taught part time any of the subjects he finds intimidating we are able to provide well constructed and clear lessons by means of cell phone MMS and SMS'es, email or Skype. We have gifted teachers who have insight into the learning behaviour of students with years of experience. A student just needs to say yes as he will not have to attend any classes. Everything is done by cell phone or Internet for those who have access to it. I have a list of extra subjects we offer and their corresponding fees on this list which I am going to leave with you."

Continue: "Before I leave, can you give me the names of three people you know whom you believe can also be interested in this service?" You will find that people are willing to help you with the names of the people they know without any problem. Then your duty will be to diarize them for your subsequent visits. Person to person approach works better than SMS system because SMS can be ignored or forgotten easily.

On Friday or appointed day you go to his work place and ask to see him at the appointed time. If you can get him to sign an enrolment form or purchase invoice on the first visit it will be much better for you to curb the change of mind scenario.

If you are faithful in doing your assignments and training as taught in this publication the law of cause and effect will send money your way. There is no other way. This law is faithful to all. The question is that are you going to be faithful too or decide to be casual about yourself employment. In this world the half-hearted get half desirable results. Ask yourself: Am I spending time apart from all distractions to plan, rehearse my presentations and analyze how I can become even more successful in this field? Meditating on each step of your work will turn this lesson into your second nature to your surprise. You will become an expert because half hearted efforts will be eliminated. These methods do work very well. They are just waiting for your input.

WAYS TO REACH POTENTIAL CLIENTS

1. ADVERTISING: Find publications that offer cheap advertisement rates. To do it right, do study other ads in the various papers to see how they word their ads. Meditate on the way they are written until you feel you can do it too by yourself.

For international readers check for similar local services you can use that provide the same services as the ones mentioned below.

2. Print flyers with your advert and premium telephone / cell phone number. Premium phone number is the number you get paid by a telephone company every time you answer your phone. To find one in your city just Goole 'Premium telephone number providers list n New York' if you live in New York.' In South Africa visit www.paytel.co.za, www.evolvingconcepts.co.za and www.free086numbers.co.za. Open an account with a good 086 company (http://www.free086numbers.co.za/) to enable you to get a premium phone number which you will distribute to your clients for them to use when they call you. For this you will need Telkom land line. PAYTEL (http://www.paytel.co.za) will give you their premium number which you will distribute to people so that they use it to call you. For this you will need a land line with TELKOM. The new premium number they give you will work without any problem or conflict with your present TELKOM land line number. This means your one handset will be able to receive calls from any of these two numbers. TELKOM number will not give any money for incoming calls. Only the new premium number from PAYTEL will pay you for every minute of all incoming calls. Vox Telecom through www.evolvingconcepts.co.za/vox/ will give you a new premium number their own ADSL line and a new handset. Registration with these companies is very much affordable. Paytel accepts only businesses while evolving concepts accepts both individuals and businesses. Visit these sites and see updated prices and conditions. If it is not convenient for you to get a premium telephone number you will need to use your cell phone number; but you will only profit from the service you provide to customers whereas the premium number would enable you to also get paid by telephone companies every time you receive a call.

This business is not suitable for people who have full time jobs because you need to answer your phone the whole day. You must advertise much to let as many people as possible know about your services so that your phone will never stop ringing with enquiries.

If you do not have money for phone connection it is not a problem. Just see clients face to face the way insurance companies' agents do. Then, when you have made enough money you can get your own land line to monetize. You can even use answering machines to let customers listen to tapes you have made that solve their problems. However, you will need to tell them on your ads that they will be listening to recordings so that they do not hang up thinking they were supposed to speak to a live person. Also, you need to disclose how long the tape takes from start to finish so that they never cut the line not knowing how long your presentation will take. This is a necessary disclosure for their budgets.

Hand out flyers by paying someone $50.00 / R50.00 per four hours per day. Target the working people while they are waiting for taxis, buses or trains in the queues after work which is from 3.00pm to 7.00pm. Target queues that are closer to each other and the next day you move to other groups of queues until you have distributed about five thousand flyers. Do stand by and monitor the worker who distributes flyers and make sure that he is aware that you are watching him. This way he will not throw them away and come to lie to you that he finished the work. Do not make him feel uneasy when passersby do not take flyers from his hand and he is left with a lot of flyers because it is not his fault. If you cannot presently afford the flyer distribution do not worry, just use other methods until you have made money to re-invest in flyer distribution. Check with Rainbow ads at www.rainbowads.co.za as they print and distribute flyers for businesses if you live in South Africa. Or search for local ads printers and distributors of flyers if you live elsewhere. If you live in

New York Google 'print and distribute New York', 'print and post New York', etc. to find the services you can use for printing and distributing your advertising flyers or brochures.

3. Go to people's homes and offices to present your product / service after making appointments.

4. You can call people on their house phones or cell phones for making appointments or to sell your product or service over the phone. The fact that there are many call canters around is a proof that a phone can feed you and your loved ones. To learn how to sell services and products through telephone just Google 'how to sell products through telephone' or other similar phrases until you

find the free lessons that satisfy your quest. Also visit www.youtube.com and type the similar phrases on search box and then click go. You will be shown many uploaded videos that teach how to prospect through telephone for free. Take notes, read them, meditate on them to see if you really get what is being taught. Then, take a few days reflecting and practicing your telephone presentation by acting as if you are actually talking to your prospect over the phone. Do not think about it, just practice it and this will pay good dividends when you are actually prospecting through telephone. By going through the motions of speaking to prospects over the phone will plant the know-how in your subconscious mind which makes it easier for you to be smooth when you are actually talking to a prospect. This will help you not to focus on finding the right words to convey your message but on effectively communicating with your prospect in order to finally make a sale. You are bound to meet rejections and rude people but it is always good to remember that their actions are not your own making and has nothing to do with you personally. It is their problem and not yours; so do not let such people derail your marketing in any way.

A WORD ON SELF EMPLOY

Self employment is very easy when you are able to approach people and ask for appointment to see them in order to introduce your product or service to them. Failure in this will ensure your failure to employ yourself. So do decide to force yourself to go through the pain of discomfort of having to approach people until it becomes a joy to you. There is no other way if you want to reach the level of those who MAKE THINGS HAPPEN. Choose to offer the product you feel would make you happy or content if it was offered to you. This way it will be easier for you to see your efforts as love and care for other people who are not yet enjoying the benefits of your product or service. Ever remember that there very many people who are like you; the people who will want what you want.

When you feel convinced that you can start approaching working people for business; you are ready to choose the product or service you will sell to them. Start by looking at all classified adverts you can lay your hands on. When you see the product or service you like you contact the advertiser by phone or email. You convince him that if he allows you to work with him you can find clients for his service or product for a flat rate you feel will be appropriate for you or on percentage basis.

For example, I convinced one nursing school owner that if he gave me $400.00 / R400.00 per student I enroll with her school; I would surely bring her students who would otherwise never come to know about her school. And he agreed because his fees were about six thousand Dollars / Rand per year; and that he would pay me only after the student I brought had paid for the school fee. I was able to bring him new students regularly. The good thing about business schools and health schools is that they are able to intake new students all year round. Or when you see an advert posted in the street, work place notice board or publication which promises to improve the level of students' performance at their respective schools on part time. You can convince the advertisers that you can speak to students who happen to be everywhere to enroll with him for weekend extra lessons or after school email system / Skype live video tuition just like correspondence schools do. Skype connects to limited number of about fifteen individual participants. So will need to set up three accounts for 45 participants with three web cameras all connected to three computers, each with its own

Skype address. Alternatively, you can get software which enables a live participation of two hundred individuals at the same time. Use search engines to find one.

Most business owners do not have the time and expertise to personally approach people and convince them to buy their services. They rely on word of mouth of satisfied customers, flyers, advertising which are good but are never as powerful as the person to person presentation. Person to person presentation is very effective because you can deal with objections to buy while adverts cannot. Your attitude, enthusiasm and your tone of voice are very important in hooking a prospect to your service or product. This approach also forces a prospect to really listen to your message and to ask questions which cannot happen with advertising. This is what creates an opportunity for you to self employ yourself at WILL while countless people are still waiting for companies to call them for interviews.

People who lack this self employment knowledge are not able to create an employ for them. They have to go through frustration of waiting and waiting for vacancies. If you can force yourself to approach prospects with your product or service you will never know the suffering of waiting in vain for vacancies. So do decide to go through the pain or discomfort of approaching strangers in order to get business from them. Your money is not on the trees; but in the pockets and bank accounts of people around you. So, first train yourself to become competent in your service and you are ready to approach them for your money. Past surveys used to show that out of every six people you approach one will definitely buy your product or service. This means if you need to sell two items or services per day you will need to make a plan to see about twelve working people per day. So you will be very busy the whole day.

This way there will never be a time when you will find yourself not working because there will never be a time business people will stop looking for new business. If you are unemployed but you desire to have money you NOW know what to do. If you desire to start but you feel 'something' unexplainable in you stopping you or preventing you to start while it does not stop you or prevent you from waiting for uncertain vacancies to; you will need to become a Christian who is connected to Christ as a branch so that His heavenly life may release you from it (that 'something' in you). Do get my free e-book titled: THE LIFE I NOW LIVE-THE

LIFE OF CHRIST THROUGH THE HOLY SPIRIT. Christ will be able to get rid of that 'something' which acts as money blockage concerning your MAKE THINGS HAPPEN attitude and habit.

SECTION THREE

HOME BUSINESSES YOU CAN START:

There are two ways in this publication that can be followed by anyone to make a living through self employment. Before we go any further I would like to stress the point that what I write concerning the three business ideas below is what has been tested over and over; and you, too, will get a proof that they do work when you follow my directives. So do not make the mistake of trying to evaluate anything because that will be to give falsehood a chance to derail you and have you end up not having done anything concrete concerning these two self employment methods. Do not try to involve your personal beliefs or views, rather, just follow to the letter what is written in this publication so that you can reap the rewards of increased finances.   Ever remember: PEOPLE FAIL BUT SYSTEMS SUCCEED. This means you need to try not to be another teacher by letting me be the teacher and you the follower or student, unless you are already making enough money for yourself or if you are not interested in self employ.

BUSINESS ONE

WORK AS A SERVICE PROVIDER

This business is an online work which you can do from your home or office. The difficult part about this method is that it requires a lot of time for learning skills that are necessary in order to provide the services that are already in demand. Let me to summarize what your duties will entail in this self employment:

1. You decide to start and operate this business
2. You visit a website where different products and services are sold for about R 80.00 each
3. You study which products are in demand by checking the length of the queues waiting to be delivered by the seller to the buyers
4. You decide to learn how you too can master the skills necessary to enable you to provide the same kind of services you noticed that they are in demand or have long queues of orders waiting to be executed by the seller
5. Decide how you are going to learn the skills necessary to be able to provide the same in demand services. As for me, I buy how -to-books from charity stores and second hand books stores. I got the following titles from charity shops: How to design a website in 24 hours; teach yourself visual basic in 21 days; Learn HTML in 25 days, etc.
6. When you are good with the skills you learned it is time to start letting buyers know about your abilities on Fiverr. You advertise your service on Fiverr.
7. Buyers will start to queue for your services too as they did to others who provide the same services as yourself
8. Try to provide at least three to five services or products per day from the queue at your door.

You will only be limited by your unwillingness to educate yourself as necessary. Now, let us get to business. Visit a website called www.fiverr.com Spend about four hours a day searching this website for sellers who have unattended orders which are still in their queues. If you cannot spend four hours a day for this you are not ready for self employment. In my case I found the following services or products waiting for sellers to fulfill them. Then you look for the courses or lessons that will help you to produce, master and provide the service(s) that have queues. When you have become competent you will need to sign up with Fiverr; and then list your services. You, too, will begin to have people starting to queue for your services also. To start searching for the software you will need to use to produce your products you will need to Google e.g. 'Logo Making software' and then buy it. If you do not have money to buy the necessary software you will need to Google 'Logo making freeware download.' Some freeware are not good and then there are those that are good. So you will need to be patient and keep searching from different freeware websites until you find the software that satisfies you. Then, you will need to study how it works and what it can do; and learn to make samples of logos of your own creation or by duplicating other people's logos you see on the various websites or publications until you can reproduce them perfectly. As you do this your proficiency will improve until you feel like an expert. That will be the time you can start selling your services.

SUMMARY: 1) you sell logos at Fiverr 2) you seek employment where you can make logos and other designs by photo editing computer programs. 3) You provide logo making service to all local businesses in your area. 4) This method can be used to sell other items that have queuing orders at the Fiverr sellers' doors. Spend time at Fiverr website to find out what services have queuing orders and then decide on the self education necessary.

BUSINESS TWO

YOU WORK AS A MIDDLEMAN

In this business you do **not** need to learn how to design any logo, website, or learn HTML, programming, etc. What you will be doing is to advertise logo making or any business in popular newspapers and magazines in your area which will be paid from your own pocket. You can also advertise your business on free classifieds websites worldwide or locally if they are available. People who respond to your advertisement will pay you upfront. You then deliver the logo after receiving it from Fiverr seller by emailing it to your client or personally delivering it. If you do not have money for advertising you must personally go to potential clients at their jobs as taught in SECTION TWO in this publication. When you supply local businesses you will be paid upon delivery. Which means you will have ordered the logo with your own money. This is risky because your client may change his mind and decide to cancel the order. But you can sell the same logo to another business and have it changed here and there to fit the specifications of the second client. You may also need to pay for the changes at any Fiverr logo maker.   The profits will cover the losses caused by cancelled orders. When you get an order you pay any Fiverr seller or designer of logos $5.00 and you supply him with the details from your client so that they can make a fitting logo according to your client's specifications concerning colours, shapes and whatever a client mentioned to you. The good part is that you can send back the logo for changes, additions or deletions your client pointed out when you delivered his logo. This you can do until the logo is just as the client requires. You then charge your client about R500.00 and your logo making cost from Fiverr seller will be about R80.00 or $5.00. Your profit will be R420.00 per logo as a middle man. Using the middle man concept you can also advertise your logo making service on your own website. When you get an order you pass it to Fiverr logo seller and then deliver it by email to your client who ordered it through your website. Some of the best selling services or products are the following; but there are many more you can see them being sold on Fiverr, which you can resell locally by visiting local businesses or worldwide through your own website or free and paid classified ads websites worldwide or locally.

1.	EBAY: Ebay is very popular and it is a platform where people worldwide use to sell anything they no longer need like used shoes, clothes and other kitchen items lying around the house unused. You advertise your items on Ebay after opening an account for selling with them. Many people make money by being affiliates of Ebay. They sell products that are sold on Ebay through their own website as middle men. When customers buy from their websites they make affiliate profits from Ebay. This means they get paid by Ebay for having brought them buyers through their websites or whatever manner they used to bring buyers to buy products from Ebay. If you learn how to make a website which list Ebay products and then you are able to insert or embed any affiliate number or identity so that people who buy from such a site get marked by Ebay as belonging to such identity or affiliate number. Many people are interested in having an affiliate website which sells for them Ebay products. This is where your self-education on how to make affiliate websites comes in. Once you master the skill of making Ebay affiliate website you are on your way to making money through Fiverr platform. There will be a queue of people at your door who want you to build them Ebay affiliate websites. If you do not wish to study how to make Ebay Affiliate websites you can sell any niche websites to local businesses. You gather the specifications for their required websites and then you pass those details to Fiverr seller and resell it back to a local business. You will need to educate local business owners on the need to have their own websites so that they can order their websites from you. You will be paying for a five or ten page website from $5.00 / R80.00 or $10.00 / R160.00 and your selling price can be about $50.00 / R700.00 or more. Check what local businesses charge and set your own prices to be lower to get more share of the market. Currently, a ten page website designers charge $5.000 / R5.000. You can advertise Ebay Affiliate website designing on your own website and then pass the orders to Fiverr seller who designs Ebay Affiliate websites for about $10.00 / R160.00 each, when you get orders. The sure way of getting orders is to actually approach the business owners personally, just as insurance representatives do. This is the most effective way of getting a lot of business because people love to buy from the person they see than send their money to remote owners of the websites.

2. WEBSITE OPTIMIZATION: Websites optimization is a hit on Fiverr because every website owner is more than willing to have his website reach the top forty on Google search engine listing. The reason is when your website is ranked / listed on the first twenty or forty the owner is easily found through search key words typed in by the seeker on Google search. When a seeker searches for Ebay Affiliate on Google search box and your website appears on the first to the fourth page you stand a good chance of getting lots of customers for your products or services. Google search engine will be helping you by sending customers your way. Now, good as it sounds, it is a very difficult undertaking to have your own website to be ranked by Google search engines in top forty listing because there are hundreds of thousands of other websites competing for higher ranking. So you need a Fiverr seller who is an expert at causing websites to rank higher in search engines. His expertise will cause most websites he attends to rank far higher than where they were before optimization; in just a few months. The reason is that he has studied very well what search engines look for when they rank websites higher and then they optimize your own website by twigging here and there and then they submit it to search engines to get it registered with them. This service is one of the hottest selling services anywhere. When you have found a proven Fiverr seller who is able to rank websites to pages 1-4 on google search engine you then advertise the 'website optimization' service on your own website or newspapers' classified ads section. When the Fiverr seller promises four months, you as the reseller you can promise up to eight months optimizing period to buy yourself enough time to rectify matters should things go wrong somewhere, like if your seller dies or is no longer able to provide the service or if Google changed their ranking algorithm to a new one which your current Fiverr seller may not be familiar with. In such cases you can seek a new seller who has caught on the new algorithm and is able to rank higher after Google changes. You should be able to give refunds when Fiverr seller's efforts fail to help your client website reach 1-4 ranking as there will be websites which will fail to rank up to page four. But in most cases it will be a successful money making business for you. The refunds will be far less and in between; and profits will make up for the loss without any problem. The ranking of websites will always be in demand because it is the dream of every website owner

to rank on the first four pages of Google search engine. When you tell your prospective clients that your company helps to rank websites for customers they will instantly be all ears to find out if you can do the same for them. After explaining to them your website optimization service you tell them the charge which will be profitable to your satisfaction; and you have a business from them. If you are lenient, website optimization will fetch for you around $300.00 / R3.000.00 minus Fiverr seller who will be optimizing your client's website to eventually rank in the first four pages of Google search engine.

Google search engine. This will be easy because you are selling a genuine service whose results everyone can see. Imagine taking a thirsty horse to a dam; it must drink. That is how easy it is to sell website optimization service.

3. WEBSITE AUCTION: One of the best methods of making money online is the selling of high ranking websites through online auctions. This is how it works. You buy a domain name and hosting for your website on any niche you decided to follow. But before you buy any domain name you will need to do a home work on finding out what website you can easily start and write a good or helpful content for, either by yourself or by hiring freelancer who will be able to provide the necessary content on a weekly basis. You also need to study what kind of websites were sold well for high returns on www.flippa.com , which is the auction website you are going to be auctioning your own optimized website(s) on. You should take into consideration your ability to provide helpful content on your website regularly and combine it with the highest possible / probable prices being paid for such niche / content websites. You do not need to figure out anything; you just need to read and see the websites that were bought for high prices. Some websites are bought for $100.000 others for $300,000 or more. This is because websites are regarded as real and serious business just as local businesses are a serious business. The more monthly visitors the website has the more money it fetches at auctions even if it makes no money at all. Those who buy will be after the idea of monetizing its traffic for themselves. The more money it makes per month the higher the auction price it commands. For instance, if a

website makes $3000.00 / R42 000.00 per month; it can be auctioned for more than $100 000.00 / R1400 000.00 before tax. Less paying websites fetch about $2.000-$12.000 which is still very good money. 1) You spend about $10.00 / R150.00 on domain name, $50.00 / R600.00 on hosting for one year. 2) you spend $300.00 / R300.00 per month on buying content from freelancing writers 3) You spend about $30.00 / R450.00 on website ranking effort by proven Fiverr seller over six months. 4) Once your website reaches 1-4 rage rank you immediately list it on www.flippa.com auction website. You will need to pay about R150.00 for listing your website to be auctioned. In my case I would buy domain name and hosting, the ranking of website to at least page four and the cost of listing on the auction website. The researching and writing of content would be done by me. If you are willing to learn how you can write your own content. You Google 'content fetching software.' You can buy or get it as a freeware. You send the software to go all over the Internet to collect the data you requested. You sift through the data it brought you and write your own content out of the content you received, which you want to write on your website. The auction website will tell you everything you need to know on what to do to auction your website successfully. You can find hosting service providers who are very cheaper than the prices above if you search for them on Google. The following points will enhance the attractiveness of your website. The name should be easily memorable one, short and end with a dot com extension. Other extensions like dot net or dot org still do sell but not like dot com ones. To come up with a good domain name, write down all the names that come to your mind; and make a list of them. The name should be somehow a short description about what your website is all about. Take as long as you feel is needed. The following day, read the names on the list to see which one(s) seem to stand out from the rest; and then if possible try to shorten them without losing their impact on your consciousness barometer. Take at last three days to finalize the choice of the domain name / website name. Keep listing and evaluating ALL the names that come to your mind until you feel that you have completed your homework to your satisfaction. On your list mark the first choice / the best name according to your gut feeling as one, the second choice as two and so forth. This you do so that if the first name is already taken when you check its availability, you go on to the second choice until you find the name that is available as you go down the list.

Note: Search for the availability of your chosen website name / domain name only when you are ready to buy it because when you type it in the availability box to see if it taken or not and then decide to buy it later; you may be giving the owners of the website you are using the chance to take that name and go on to sell it elsewhere as just a domain name and they will make more money than if you bought it from them. You will have given them the idea which they may unscrupulously take and use to make extra money. And the next time you come and try to register it you find that it is already taken. You will need a credit card to purchase whatever you want to purchase; and a bank account to receive the money from auction purchases. If you do not qualify for credit card from your local banks you can get one from www.payoneer.com . It will take about three weeks for you to receive their international master card through the post. But it works like a prepaid card; so you will not get any credit or overdraft for any reason. That is the reason why it is available to everyone who wants it; more over it is free. Again, the prices above are just for giving the reader a rough idea; the actual costs will vary according to different service providers.

PART TWO

KING SOLOMON'S FIVE MONEY SECRETS
YOU CAN DUPLICATE

INTRODUCTION

If you follow the secrets in this publication your life is sure to take an upward turn for the better. You will be able to control your funds joyfully as you cover all your needs and your loved ones' needs. The following advice consists of workable principles that work every time they are employed. Success is achieved by constantly applying success principles day after day, week after week, month after month and year after year. Success principles do not discriminate between persons, instead they work for every person who will understand them and apply them as required to produce desired results of material acquisition. There are five things that will stop you from reaching your material goals. These are:

1) If you half half-heartedly apply success principles because success is not easy for people who are lazy or undecided.

2) If you apply success principles together with your own untested and unproven beliefs and actions. Your unproven beliefs concerning success will short-circuit the power of success principles. The secret is to follow success principles and strategies without going to the left or right as if you are programmed like a robot.

3) If you are not ready to protect your gains with all your might. Achieving success is not as difficult as maintaining it. The reason is that success attracts wrong people to you who will borrow from and never return, steal from you, seduce you for the sake of spending and enjoying your money; cast anti-success spells against you, not to mention new friends whose intentions is to suck on your wealth and leave you dry.

4) If you pursue more than one goal your brain power and push will be thinly divided which in turn cause you to fail to reach your goal. The secret is to

live by this principle: 'Single mindedness guarantees success, period.'

5) If you are hexed because you are not spiritually protected from the dark forces. You must be prepared for people who are against your success because some of them know how to send success-destroying spirits your way. This happens in all races and nationalities.   In my observation, this is what effectively blocks our African continent from becoming the first world continent.

SECRET ONE

Cast off weight from your money power:

a) Stop purchasing items on hire purchase as it is based on greed of obtaining what you do not yet qualify to own. Hire purchase is alright for people who are not experiencing money problems. The result is you pay too much. Learn to buy on lay-buy method. Your patience will save thousands which you can invest to make your money grow. Forget about social pride, peer pressure or unannounced competition among your friends. Soon they will begin to envy you when these methods take you to new heights right before their eyes. Decide from today to use a different system of acquiring things and forget what people will say. The true wisdom is seen by abundance of fruit; not struggle to keep your head above the water. You owe it to yourself and your loved ones.

b) Stop paying other people's debts including your sons' / daughters' debts if they are working but are spending their money elsewhere other than on their responsibilities. Your children are yours but they are not your adults. They are no longer your obligation because they need to reap what they sow; this is the will of God for everyone who decides to live carelessly despite good advice and guidance given to them.

c) Make it your habit to buy clothes when they are on sale. If you wait patiently the clothes you saw and decided to get will soon be on sale. Give a sales lady your cell phone number so that she can let you know when there is a sale at their store. Promise her a free lunch when she calls you as a thank you gift because she is saving you a fortune.

d) Locate cheaper products directly from manufacturers or wholesalers who are able to sell one item without forcing you to buy in bulk. Before you buy any cutlery, electronic equipment, furniture or ornaments browse the World Wide Web (Internet) to see if what you want you can get from manufacturers or wholesalers. For instance, if you decide to buy a hand bag or laptop you type on your browser / address space on the Internet something like: "Italian ladies hand bags manufacturers wholesalers" If you do not seek specifically Italian bag just leave out the word "Italian". For laptops you type something like: "laptop manufacturers wholesalers" For the safety of your money choose suppliers who use pay pal payment method or credit card payment method because the charges can be reversed if what you received is not what you ordered. Pay Pal now has this service. Better still use en screw payment method with the companies which accepts such payment. En crew payment means you send the money for the product you order to a neutral third party who specializes as en screw. He keeps the money until you confirm that you have received your order and are satisfied that it works well. Then the supplier gets his money from the escrow you used. Escrow Company gets a small percentage for protecting your money this way. Many manufacturers in China and Hong Kong and worldwide use this payment method to proof that they are confident in their products and are not out to scam or cheat people. To get addresses of en screwing companies you type on the browser: Reliable Es crew companies or good en crew payment dealer. This way a laptop which sells for R3.000.00 locally you get for R1200.00 postage included and your order will arrive in two to three weeks through the post. You must ask them to use registered shipping so that your order may not get lost during shipping. This way you should easily be able to acquire possessions which will make you an envy of your neighbors. And you will have extra money to test and really invest in profitable investment vehicles.

Meditate on this verse: "Better is he who is lightly esteemed, and has a servant; than he who honors himself, and lacks bread." Proverbs 12:19.

SECRET TWO:

The right attitude towards money:

The second secret is to have the right attitude towards money. When you receive a salary or money do not go out to spend it on desires you find enjoyable. The rule is to stay calm, cool and collected. Stand still and let the needs be the ones that come to fetch the money from you. Not you, going out after them. King Solomon says when a fool or ignorant person gets money he starts off in all directions to fulfill his desires. He says human desires are like graves because they are never satisfied or have enough. This tells us that going after our desires instead of genuine needs causes our money to be divided. Together we stand, divided we fall is the truth which applies to our money also. The less desires we fulfill with our money and concentrate its power to a few most important needs the more power it will have of getting us out of our financial struggle into financial independence.

Here is what we mean by stand still and let genuine needs be the ones which get money from you. When a wise person gets money he continues to do things the same way he was doing them BEFORE he received the salary/money. The presence of money in his bank account or pocket does not prod him to go out to spend it. It does not breed all kinds of spending impulses which cause him to have no rest; and to toss and turn at night instead of sleeping when he thinks of what he could be doing with the money. Instead, it fills him with pleasure and a sense of self worth. The solution is: WHAT WERE YOU DOING BEFORE MONEY CAME? What were you going to eat, do and never do if your salary never came? Write them down and decide to continue with them as if your salary has not been received. Learn to act as if you have not received any money; and pay only for things that need you to pay for like rent, illness and school fees. These are not wants or desires but genuine needs. Forget about joining friends for money spending entertainment and other pleasures because it is time for sacrifice for the sake of your future enjoyment and much desired financial independence. Your target should be to reach the state where your money will start to work for you, instead of you working for your money for a change. Are you prepared to pay the price this way in exchange for your brighter future for your sake and for the sake of your loved ones and your own children? By following this secret you too can become a hero to your children and die having gained their respect and admiration for you. The choice is yours. Stop going after your wants which come to your attention disguised as needs. Put to practice this secret for the first month and you will be surprised how much money will still be there in your bank account when the next payday arrives. And remember: You first make the habit and later that habit will make you. In other words after two to four months of practicing this way of living you will begin to find it hard to stop it and go back to the old foolish way of living.

Meditate on these verses of wisdom: Live by the second part of this verse: "Some pretend to be rich, but have nothing. There are those who pretend to have nothing but are rich." Proverbs 13:7 He who gathers in summer is a wise son." Proverbs 10:5, Just as Sheol and Abaddon are never satisfied, so are a man's eyes; they are never satisfied." Proverbs 27:20

SECRET THREE:

Protect your money by eliminating your spending weaknesses.

The third secret is to master self control when it comes to money matters. Check your SELF to see which of the character leaks you suffer from. By character leaks I mean the habit(s) which cause you to lose money in unplanned or undesirable manner. Is picnicking, gambling, drinking, partying, clubbing, sporting, adulterating or any endeavor somehow, one way or another causes you to spend more money than you had planned? If your answer is "yes" then you are a leaking character and you need to remedy the situation because there is no way you can climb your way up to financial independence. You are like a mad person who keeps carrying water using a bucket with many big or small holes at the bottom. You are indeed controlled by subhuman tendencies which need you to take remedying action immediately. Do not just plan to seek solution to your leakage but do choose a day, and write it in your diary, you will go out to seek help if you cannot do it on your own. Then when that chosen day comes go and get the solution you decided upon.

If you buy things on impulse and regret it later, feel uncomfortable when there is money in your bank account (something inside you cries or demands that you go out to spend it or else you never know rest in any way), borrow money for entertainment, feel sorry for people to the extent of paying for their needs in not budgeted manner; you MUST set a date to see a social worker because you need help real quick. You need a hand which will help to pull you out of your dungeon. If drinking is the cause of your wild spending you MUST seek a doctor who can help you with your addiction because it is your weakest link or you can join Alcohol Anonymous in your area. People like you have been helped. Blue Cross also helps people who suffer addictions including drugs. Or you can do your best to get my book called: "THE LIFE I NOW LIVE-THE LIFE OF CHRIST THROUGH THE HOLY SPIRT". In this book, I show how Christ can literally (in the way you can feel) remove your addictions by replacing your weaknesses with His overcoming strength. You will be helped even if you do not attend any church. Your loved ones and children will feel fortunate to have you in their lives. So do take the necessary action immediately for their sake. Give them the GIFT of joy and happiness they deserve.

Meditate on the following verses: "Drink water out of your own cistern, running water out of your own well...Should your springs overflow in the streets, the streams of water in the public square? Let them be for yourself alone, not for strangers with you." Proverbs 5:15-17 "Be not responsible for others' debts." Proverbs 11: 15, "He who loves pleasure shall be a poor man. He who loves wine and oil shall not be rich." Proverbs 21:17, "There is precious treasure in the dwelling of the wise; but a foolish man swallows it up". Proverbs 21: 20.

SECRET FOUR:

Get into agriculture, manufacture, import or export business.

Find something to export or import or mass produce for merchants so that you make money from it. Importing requires business registration, import permit and a rented business premises. Any time you hear someone complain about life's adversities make it your business to find a product or service which can eradicate such problem and seek a way to supply it for a profit either by affiliating, drop shipping or by buying and reselling for a profit. On your Internet browser you just type on search line whatever you want know. You can be sure that somewhere someone has already written a book on it. There is no solution you cannot find from the Internet. Do ask Internet shop worker for assistance if you are not yet familiar with it. Just ask him to show you how you can search for it. Alternatively, you can find something(s) made locally which you can export. Search on the Internet the foreign shops, businesses which sell similar or related product(s) in their countries to whatever product(s) you wish to export. Whatever you feel you can buy for yourself is the right choice because there are millions of people like you; namely, who can / want to buy it / them. You can make your own product or service according to what talent you believe you have.

If you do not like selling you can invest in shares which are affordable and have little risk of reducing your invested money. If you are like me you will want to learn more on the following investments: Penny Shares, stocks and commodities. Just search them from the Internet. As a matter of rule do not buy or participate in a program which promises you easy money by believing in the words of the advertisement until you have found about it from more than one review sites; to hear from third parties who used the program. Only when the results the participants got match the rich promises from the advert can you buy. This is the way to avoid being scammed. To get to review sites type on the search space on the Internet words like "independent review site then the word(s) referring to what you want to learn about its review. For example: independent penny shares review / www.workfromhomejobs review. Adding the word *review* after the address with its extension will take you to reviews by the company you want to know about. The problem with this is that no company can tell an honest review when it reviews itself. An example of adding the word 'review' after the extension is: "http://www.workfromhomejobs.com/ review.

What is it you can make? Can you bake; make a special or loved drink? Can you knit, sow or have any thing you can skillfully do? Then get someone to market it for you to merchants. You can find such persons from insurance companies. You will need to first agree on the amount of commission you are going to give him or her on every order. There are some who will agree to seek orders for your items from the merchants who are going to resell your items in their shops. Do not try to sell to the public by yourself as you will make little money; which will in turn make it hard or impossible for you to reach a stage where your money will start working for you through investments. Merchants buy in bulk and pay cash. If you lack capital for material you can use the filled order form or invoice from the merchant who was convinced to buy by your sales person and take it to your bank manager. Show him the order and ask him for a loan; and that you will have the money paid directly into your bank account so that the bank can withdraw its money plus interest before you can get access to the money. Under this circumstance you should be able to get a loan. If you cannot get it due to some reason make it a point to buy seeds for tomato, green paper and find out which other vegetables are profitable. I happen to know this two personally.

At the right time to start sowing them, plant them using composed you bought or made by yourself. Your school child will know how to make it or go to agricultural department and they should be able to help you with the knowledge on how to make it. One plant of pepper will give you about $30.00 per month from the spring season to the beginning of winter. (This is about seven months. Start with at least two hundred or one hundred plants at about one foot (30 cm) apart. They will need a space of about one average room. Most importantly, find the name of the well tested and tried chemical which will keep worms and other parasites from your plants; and follow instructions precisely. Surely, you can have this amount of space in your yard. Simply go to supermarket in your area and ask them to order from you to supply them with pepper or tomato for the next seven or six months. After agreeing on the price you are set to start accumulating capital for your bigger job. Do not let greed or your desire to get rich make you set high prices because God may be forced to make you fail. How much do you stand to make? $30 by 100 = $3000 per month by 7 months = $21,000.00 If you have no money for seeds and a space to plant you can overcome this by finding someone who has both the money and the space to partner with you. You will be supplying expertise and hands on as your contribution. And you agree to share the money 50/50. Think bigger by getting more deals as long as you will be able to maintain their smooth and profitable running. If you are smart you can run four such projects with four different people. This could mean $10,500 by 4= $42,000 per year for you using only your mouth and hands. Work only with people who will have no problem signing the deal on paper. Forget those who ask you to trust them without signing anything on paper. They are not worth your trouble.

Meditate on these words: She makes linen garments and sells them, and supplies merchants with sashes. Proverbs 31: 24, "She considers a field and buys it; out of her earnings." Proverbs 31:16; "So are the ways of everyone who is greedy for a gain. It takes away the life of its owner." Proverbs 1:19.

SECRET FIVE:

This secret is all about removing unexpected and unforeseen obstacles that prevent you from succeeding with your endeavors to reach your goals. You may read this manual and understand the contents but still fail to put them to practice without knowing the reason why. You may be brilliant and have all life enriching knowledge and still be very unsuccessful. Some people call this bad luck or bewitchment. For me I call it LACK of blessings. If your plans are always thwarted by unexpected and unavoidable expenses or emergencies which keep groping up every time you get money to block you way to success then this secret will release you immediately. Do you say: I get money but I cannot tell you exactly how it vanishes or where it goes? No amount of evil spells against you will stop your success when you forget your personal views and start living under the protection of this secret.

Here is the secret: Find one or two people who you know that they are truly struggling and are always in need. It is not hard to recall poor people you are aware of in your community or elsewhere. Agree with him or her that you want to provide him with food every time you get your salary or profits from your business for five months or so; according to your choice. The reason being you may need to change the recipients after a while. Make sure that whatever you do that you do not make a promise but an expression of your willingness to help so that he may not hold you guilty when, for any reason, you change your mind or fail to deliver according to your word. Ask him what grocery items he needs; plan together and then deliver. If he is an African you may decide on maize meal, ointment, cooking oil, sugar, salt, soap, cabbage and good soup. Do not buy him the cheap one you yourself do not enjoy because you want the best for yourself also. Do not reason or try to speculate. Just do it. I repeat for the sake of your loved ones and children: JUST DO IT. DO NOT WAIT UNTIL YOU HAVE ENOUGH MONEY TO SPARE BEFORE YOU START. It will cost you more if you do not do it than if you do it. So do not be like someone who decides to eat seed instead of planting it for far greater abundance. Are you going to plant the seed or are going to eat it? The choice is now yours. You cannot have more reasoning powers than King Solomon. Not in this life. So humble yourself under his wisdom for living because it is the wisdom directly from God, the creator of heaven and earth.

Meditate on these verses: "Honor God with your substance, with the first fruit of all your increase." Proverbs 3:27-28; Also Proverbs 3:9-10. "There is one who scatters, and increases yet more. There is one who withholds more than is appropriate, but gains poverty." Proverbs 11:24; "He who has pity (gives) on the poor lends to the Lord; He will repay him." Proverbs 19:17; one who give to the poor have no lack; but one who closes his eyes will have many curses." Proverbs 28:27.

There, I have given you five secrets from the wisest man who ever lived, King Solomon, which will make it hard for you to fail to attain the pinnacle of success. This does not mean you will get rich but it does mean your life will improve, become better and more enjoyable when you decide to listen to God who is speaking to you today through the wisdom He gave to King Solomon for the sake of all human beings.

YOU NOW HAVE WHAT THE DOCTOR ORDERED FOR MONEY MATTERS!